EASY BREAD MACHINE RECIPES

Amaze your guests with quick and easy Bread Machine Recipes!

Anna Allen

Table of Contents

Spice And Herb Breads

Oregano Mozza-Cheese Bread

Preparation Time: 15 minutes

Cooking Time: 3 hours and 15 minutes

Servings: 16 slices

Difficulty : Intermediate

Ingredients:

- 1 cup (milk + egg) mixture

- ½ cup mozzarella cheese

- 2¼ cups flour

- ¾ cup whole grain flour

- 2 tablespoons sugar

- 1 teaspoon salt

- 2 teaspoons oregano

- 1½ teaspoons dry yeast

Directions:

1. Add all of the ingredients to your bread machine, carefully following the instructions of the manufacturer.

2. Set the program of your bread machine to Basic/White Bread and set crust type to Dark.

3. Wait until the cycle completes.

4. Once the loaf is ready, take the bucket out and let the loaf cool for 5 minutes.

5. Gently shake the bucket to remove the loaf.

Nutrition:

Total Carbs: 40g

Fiber: 1g

Protein: 7.7g

Fat: 2.1g

Calories: 209

Cumin Tossed Fancy Bread

Preparation Time: 5 minutes

Cooking Time: 3 hours and 15 minutes

Servings: 16 slices

Difficulty : Intermediate

Ingredients:

- 5 1/3 cups wheat flour

- 1½ teaspoons salt

- 1½ tablespoons sugar

- 1 tablespoon dry yeast

- 1¾ cups water

- 2 tablespoons cumin

- 3 tablespoons sunflower oil

Directions:

1. Add warm water to the bread machine bucket.

2. Add salt, sugar, and sunflower oil.

3. Sift in wheat flour and add yeast.

4. Set the program of your bread machine to French bread and set crust type to Medium.

5. Once the maker beeps, add cumin.

6. Wait until the cycle completes.

7. Once the loaf is ready, take the bucket out and let the loaf cool for 5 minutes.

8. Gently shake the bucket to remove the loaf.

Nutrition:

Total Carbs: 67g

Fiber: 2g

Protein: 9.5g

Fat: 7g

Calories: 368

Potato Rosemary Loaf

Preparation Time: 5 minutes

Cooking Time: 3 hours and 25 minutes

Servings: 20 slices

Difficulty : Intermediate

Ingredients:

- 4 cups wheat flour

- 1 tablespoon sugar

- 1 tablespoon sunflower oil

- 1½ teaspoons salt

- 1½ cups water

- 1 teaspoon dry yeast

- 1 cup mashed potatoes, ground through a sieve

- crushed rosemary to taste

Directions:

1. Add flour, salt, and sugar to the bread maker bucket and attach mixing paddle.

2. Add sunflower oil and water.

3. Put in yeast as directed.

4. Set the program of your bread machine to Bread with Filling mode and set crust type to Medium.

5. Once the bread maker beeps and signals to add more ingredients, open lid, add mashed potatoes, and chopped rosemary.

6. Wait until the cycle completes.

7. Once the loaf is ready, take the bucket out and let the loaf cool for 5 minutes.

8. Gently shake the bucket to remove the loaf.

Nutrition:

Total Carbs: 54g

Fiber: 1g

Protein: 8g

Fat: 3g

Calories: 276

Delicious Honey Lavender Bread

Preparation Time: 10 minutes

Cooking Time: 3 hours and 25 minutes

Servings: 16 slices

Difficulty : Intermediate

Ingredients:

- 1½ cups wheat flour

- 2 1/3 cups whole meal flour

- 1 teaspoon fresh yeast

- 1½ cups water

- 1 teaspoon lavender

- 1½ tablespoons honey

- 1 teaspoon salt

Directions:

1. Sift both types of flour in a bowl and mix.

2. Add all of the ingredients to your bread machine, carefully following the instructions of the manufacturer.

3. Set the program of your bread machine to Basic/White Bread and set crust type to Medium.

4. Wait until the cycle completes.

5. Once the loaf is ready, take the bucket out and let the loaf cool for 5 minutes.

6. Gently shake the bucket to remove the loaf.

Nutrition:

Total Carbs: 46g

Fiber: 1g

Protein: 7.5g

Fat: 1.5g

Calories: 226

Inspiring Cinnamon Bread

Preparation Time: 15 minutes

Cooking Time: 2 hours and 15 minutes

Servings: 8 slices

Difficulty : Intermediate

Ingredients:

- 2/3 cup milk at 80 degrees F

- 1 whole egg, beaten

- 3 tablespoons melted butter, cooled

- 1/3 cup sugar

- 1/3 teaspoon salt

- 1 teaspoon ground cinnamon

- 2 cups white bread flour

- 1 1/3 teaspoons active dry yeast

Directions:

1. Add all of the ingredients to your bread machine, carefully following the instructions of the manufacturer.

2. Set the program of your bread machine to Basic/White Bread and set crust type to Medium.

3. Wait until the cycle completes.

4. Once the loaf is ready, take the bucket out and let the loaf cool for 5 minutes.

5. Remove the loaf

Nutrition:

Total Carbs: 34g

Fiber: 1g

Protein: 5g

Fat: 5g

Calories: 198

Lavender Buttermilk Bread

Preparation time: 10 minutes

Cooking time: 3 hours

Servings: 14

Difficulty : Expert

Ingredients:

- ½ cup water

- 7/8 cup buttermilk

- 1/4 cup olive oil

- 3 Tablespoon finely chopped fresh lavender leaves

- 1 ¼ teaspoon finely chopped fresh lavender flowers

- Grated zest of 1 lemon

- 4 cups bread flour

- 2 teaspoon salt

- 2 3/4 teaspoon bread machine yeast

Directions:

1. Add each ingredient to the bread machine in the order and at the temperature recommended by your bread machine manufacturer.

2. Close the lid, select the basic bread, medium crust setting on your bread machine and press start.

3. When the bread machine has finished baking, remove the bread and put it on a cooling rack.

4.

Nutrition:

Carbs: 27 g

Fat: 5 g

Protein: 2 g

Calories: 170

Cajun Bread

Preparation time: 10 minutes

Cooking time: 2 hours 10 minutes

Servings: 14

Difficulty : Intermediate

Ingredients:

- ½ cup water

- ¼ cup chopped onion

- ¼ cup chopped green bell pepper

- 2 teaspoon finely chopped garlic

- 2 teaspoon soft butter

- 2 cups bread flour

- 1 Tablespoon sugar

- 1 teaspoon Cajun

- ½ teaspoon salt

- 1 teaspoon active dry yeast

Directions

1. Add each ingredient to the bread machine in the order and at the temperature recommended by your bread machine manufacturer.

2. Close the lid, select the basic bread, medium crust setting on your bread machine and press start.

3. When the bread machine has finished baking, remove the bread and put it on a cooling rack.

Nutrition:

Carbs: 23 g

Fat: 4 g

Protein: 5 g

Calories: 150

Turmeric Bread

Preparation time: 5 minutes

Cooking time: 3 hours

Servings: 14

Difficulty : Intermediate

Ingredients:

- 1 teaspoon dried yeast

- 4 cups strong white flour

- 1 teaspoon turmeric powder

- 2 teaspoon beetroot powder

- 2 Tablespoon olive oil

- 1.5 teaspoon salt

- 1 teaspoon chili flakes

- 1 3/8 water

Directions:

1. Add each ingredient to the bread machine in the order and at the temperature recommended by your bread machine manufacturer.

2. Close the lid, select the basic bread, medium crust setting on your bread machine and press start.

3. When the bread machine has finished baking, remove the bread and put it on a cooling rack.

Nutrition:

Carbs: 24 g

Fat: 3 g

Protein: 2 g

Calories: 129

Rosemary Cranberry Pecan Bread

Preparation time: 30 minutes

Cooking time: 3 hours

Servings: 14

Difficulty : Intermediate

Ingredients:

- 1 1/3 cups water, plus

- 2 Tablespoon water

- 2 Tablespoon butter

- 2 teaspoon salt

- 4 cups bread flour

- 3/4 cup dried sweetened cranberries

- 3/4 cup toasted chopped pecans

- 2 Tablespoon non-fat powdered milk

- ¼ cup sugar

- 2 teaspoon yeast

Directions:

1. Add each ingredient to the bread machine in the order and at the temperature recommended by your bread machine manufacturer.

2. Close the lid, select the basic bread, medium crust setting on your bread machine and press start.

3. When the bread machine has finished baking, remove the bread and put it on a cooling rack.

Nutrition:

Carbs: 18 g

Fat: 5 g

Protein: 9 g

Calories: 120

Sesame French Bread

Preparation time: 20 minutes

Cooking time: 3 hours 15 minutes

Servings: 14

Difficulty : Intermediate

Ingredients:

- 7/8 cup water

- 1 Tablespoon butter, softened

- 3 cups bread flour

- 2 teaspoon sugar

- 1 teaspoon salt

- 2 teaspoon yeast

- 2 Tablespoon sesame seeds toasted

Directions:

1. Add each ingredient to the bread machine in the order and at the temperature recommended by your bread machine manufacturer.

2. Close the lid, select the French bread, medium crust setting on your bread machine and press start.

3. When the bread machine has finished baking, remove the bread and put it on a cooling rack.

Nutrition:

Carbs: 28 g

Fat: 3 g

Protein: 6 g

Calories: 180

Grain, Seed & Nut Bread

Sunflower & Flax Seed Bread

Preparation Time: 5 minutes

Cooking Time: 3 hours

Servings: 10 slices

Difficulty : Beginners

Ingredients:

- Water – 1 1/3 cups.

- Butter – 2 tablespoons.

- Honey – 3 tablespoons.

- Bread flour – 1 ½ cups.

- Whole wheat flour – 1 1/3 cups.

- Salt – 1 teaspoon.

- Active dry yeast – 1 teaspoon.

- Flax seeds – ½ cup.

- Sunflower seeds – ½ cup.

Directions:

1. Add all ingredients except for sunflower seeds into the bread machine pan.

2. Select basic setting then select light/medium crust and press start.

3. Add sunflower seeds just before the final kneading cycle.

4. Once loaf is done, remove the loaf pan from the machine. Allow it to cool for 10 minutes. Slice and serve.

Nutrition:

Calories 220,

Carbs 36.6g,

Fat 5.7g,

Protein 6.6g

Nutritious 9-Grain Bread

Preparation Time: 5 minutes

Cooking Time: 2 hours

Servings: 10 slices

Difficulty : Beginners

Ingredients:

- Warm water – 3/4 cup+2 tablespoons.

- Whole wheat flour – 1 cup.

- Bread flour – 1 cup.

- 9-grain cereal – ½ cup., crushed

- Salt – 1 teaspoon.

- Butter – 1 tablespoon.

- Sugar – 2 tablespoons.

- Milk powder – 1 tablespoon.

- Active dry yeast – 2 teaspoons.

Directions:

1. Put all ingredients into the bread machine.

2. Select whole wheat setting then select light/medium crust and start.

3. Once loaf is done, remove the loaf pan from the machine.

4. Allow it to cool for 10 minutes. Slice and serve.

Nutrition:

Calories 132,

Carbs 25g,

Fat 1.7g,

Protein 4.1g

Oatmeal Sunflower Bread

Preparation Time: 15 minutes

Cooking Time: 3 hours 30 minutes

Servings: 10 slices

Difficulty : Beginners

Ingredients:

- Water – 1 cup.

- Honey – ¼ cup.

- Butter – 2 tablespoons., softened

- Bread flour – 3 cups.

- Old fashioned oats – ½ cup.

- Milk powder – 2 tablespoons.

- Salt – 1 ¼ teaspoons.

- Active dry yeast – 2 ¼ teaspoons.

- Sunflower seeds – ½ cup.

Directions:

1. Add all ingredients except for sunflower seeds into the bread machine pan.

2. Select basic setting then select light/medium crust and press start. Add sunflower seeds just before the final kneading cycle.

3. Once loaf is done, remove the loaf pan from the machine. Allow it to cool for 10 minutes. Slice and serve.

Nutrition:

Calories 215,

Carbs 39.3g,

Fat 4.2g,

Protein 5.4g

Cornmeal Whole Wheat Bread

Preparation Time: 10 minutes

Cooking Time: 2 hours

Servings: 10 slices

Difficulty : Beginners

Ingredients:

- Active dry yeast – 2 ½ teaspoons.

- Water – 1 1/3 cups.

- Sugar – 2 tablespoons.

- Egg – 1, lightly beaten

- Butter – 2 tablespoons.

- Salt – 1 ½ teaspoons.

- Cornmeal – 3/4 cup.

- Whole wheat flour – 3/4 cup.

- Bread flour – 2 3/4 cups.

Directions:

1. Add all ingredients to the bread machine pan according to the bread machine manufacturer instructions.

2. Select basic bread setting then select medium crust and start. Once loaf is done, remove the loaf pan from the machine.

3. Allow it to cool for 10 minutes. Slice and serve.

Nutrition:

Calories 228,

Carbs 41.2g,

Fat 3.3g,

Protein 7.1g

Delicious Cranberry Bread

Preparation Time: 5 minutes

Cooking Time: 3 hours 27 minutes

Servings: 10 slices

Difficulty : Beginners

Ingredients:

- Warm water – 1 ½ cups

- Brown sugar – 2 tablespoons.

- Salt – 1 ½ teaspoons.

- Olive oil – 2 tablespoons.

- Flour – 4 cups

- Cinnamon – 1 ½ teaspoons.

- Cardamom – 1 ½ teaspoons.

- Dried cranberries – 1 cup

- Yeast – 2 teaspoons.

Directions:

1. Put all ingredients to the bread machine in the listed order.

2. Select sweet bread setting then select light/medium crust and start. Once loaf is done, remove the loaf pan from the machine.

3. Allow it to cool for 20 minutes. Slice and serve.

Nutrition:

Calories 223,

Carbs 41.9g,

Fat 3.3g,

Protein 5.5g

Coffee Raisin Bread

Preparation Time: 15 minutes

Cooking Time: 3 hours

Servings: 10 slices

Difficulty : Beginners

Ingredients:

- Active dry yeast – 2 ½ teaspoons.

- Ground cloves – ¼ teaspoon.

- Ground allspice – ¼ teaspoon.

- Ground cinnamon – 1 teaspoon.

- Sugar – 3 tablespoons.

- Egg – 1, lightly beaten

- Olive oil – 3 tablespoons.

- Strong brewed coffee – 1 cup.

- Bread flour – 3 cups.

- Raisins – 3/4 cup.

- Salt – 1 ½ teaspoons.

Directions:

1. Add all ingredients except for raisins into the bread machine pan.

2. Select basic setting then select light/medium crust and press start. Add raisins just before the final kneading cycle.

3. Once loaf is done, remove the loaf pan from the machine. Allow it to cool for 10 minutes. Slice and serve.

Nutrition:

Calories 230,

Carbs 41.5g,

Fat 5.1g,

Protein 5.2g

Healthy Multigrain Bread

Preparation Time: 5 minutes

Cooking Time: 40 minutes

Servings: 10 slices

Difficulty : Beginners

Ingredients:

- Water – 1 ¼ cups.

- Butter – 2 tablespoons.

- Bread flour – 1 1/3 cups.

- Whole wheat flour – 1 ½ cups.

- Multigrain cereal – 1 cup.

- Brown sugar – 3 tablespoons.

- Salt – 1 ¼ teaspoons.

- Yeast – 2 ½ teaspoons.

Directions:

1. Put ingredients listed into the bread machine pan. Select basic bread setting then select light/medium crust and start.

2. Once loaf is done, remove the loaf pan from the machine. Allow it to cool for 10 minutes. Slice and serve.

Nutrition:

Calories 159,

Carbs 29.3g,

Fat 2.9g,

Protein 4.6g

Italian Pine Nut Bread

Preparation Time: 5 minutes

Cooking Time: 3 hours 30 minutes

Servings: 10 slices

Difficulty : Beginners

Ingredients:

- Water – 1 cup+ 2 tablespoons.

- Bread flour – 3 cups.

- Sugar – 2 tablespoons.

- Salt – 1 teaspoon.

- Active dry yeast – 1 1/4 teaspoons.

- Basil pesto – 1/3 cup.

- Flour – 2 tablespoons.

- Pine nuts – 1/3 cup.

Directions:

1. In a small container, combine basil pesto and flour and mix until well blended. Add pine nuts and stir well. Add water, bread flour, sugar, salt, and yeast into the bread machine pan.

2. Select basic setting then select medium crust and press start. Add basil pesto mixture just before the final kneading cycle.

3. Once loaf is done, remove the loaf pan from the machine. Allow it to cool for 10 minutes. Slice and serve.

Nutrition:

Calories 180,

Carbs 32.4g,

Fat 3.5g,

Protein 4.8g

Whole Wheat Raisin Bread

Preparation Time: 5 minutes

Cooking Time: 2 hours

Servings: 10 slices

Difficulty : Beginners

Ingredients:

- Whole wheat flour – 3 ½ cups

- Dry yeast – 2 teaspoons.

- Eggs – 2, lightly beaten

- Butter – ¼ cup, softened

- Water – 3/4 cup

- Milk – 1/3 cup

- Salt – 1 teaspoon.

- Sugar – 1/3 cup

- Cinnamon – 4 teaspoons.

- Raisins – 1 cup

Directions:

1. Add water, milk, butter, and eggs to the bread pan. Add remaining ingredients except for yeast to the bread pan.

2. Make a small hole into the flour with your finger and add yeast to the hole. Make sure yeast will not be mixed with any liquids.

3. Select whole wheat setting then select light/medium crust and start. Once loaf is done, remove the loaf pan from the machine.

4. Allow it to cool for 10 minutes. Slice and serve.

Nutrition:

Calories 290,

Carbs 53.1g,

Fat 6.2g,

Protein 6.8g

Healthy Spelt Bread

Preparation Time: 15 minutes

Cooking Time: 40 minutes

Servings: 10 slices

Difficulty : Beginners

Ingredients:

- Milk – 1 ¼ cups.

- Sugar – 2 tablespoons.

- Olive oil – 2 tablespoons.

- Salt – 1 teaspoon.

- Spelt flour – 4 cups.

- Yeast – 2 ½ teaspoons.

Directions:

1. Add all ingredients according to the bread machine manufacturer instructions into the bread machine.

2. Select basic bread setting then select light/medium crust and start. Once loaf is done, remove the loaf pan from the machine.

3. Allow it to cool for 10 minutes. Slice and serve.

Nutrition:

Calories 223,

Carbs 40.3g,

Fat 4.5g,

Protein 9.2g

Awesome Rosemary Bread

Preparation Time: 5 minutes

Cooking Time: 2 hours

Servings: 8 slices

Difficulty: Beginners

Ingredients:

- 3/4 cup + 1 tablespoon water at 80 degrees F

- 1 2/3 tablespoons melted butter, cooled

- 2 teaspoons sugar

- 1 teaspoon salt

- 1 tablespoon fresh rosemary, chopped

- 2 cups white bread flour

- 1 1/3 teaspoons instant yeast

Directions:

1. Combine all of the ingredients to your bread machine, carefully following the instructions of the manufacturer.

2. Set the program of your bread machine to Basic/White Bread and set crust type to Medium.

3. Press START.

4. Wait until the cycle completes.

5. Once the loaf is ready, take the bucket out and allow the loaf to chill for 5 minutes.

6. Gently jiggle the bucket to take out the loaf.

Nutrition:

Total Carbs: 25g

Fiber: 1g

Protein: 4g

Fat: 3g

Calories: 142

Breakfast & White Breads

Basic White Bread

Preparation time: 5 minutes

Cooking time: 3 hours

Servings: 16

Difficulty : Beginners

Ingredients:

- 1 cup warm water (about 110ºF/45ºC)

- 2 Tablespoon sugar

- 2¼ teaspoon (.25-ounce package) bread machine yeast

- ¼ cup rice bran oil

- 3 cups bread flour

- 1 teaspoon salt

Directions:

1. Add each ingredient to the bread machine in the order and at the temperature recommended by your bread machine manufacturer.

2. Close the lid, select the basic or white bread, low crust setting on your bread machine, and press start.

3. When the bread machine has finished baking, remove the bread and put it on a cooling rack.

Nutrition:

Carbs: 18 g

Fat: 1 g

Protein: 3 g

Calories: 95

Extra Buttery White Bread

Preparation time: 10 minutes

Cooking time: 3 hours 10 minutes

Servings: 16

Difficulty : Beginners

Ingredients:

- 1 1/8 cups milk

- 4 Tablespoon unsalted butter

- 3 cups bread flour

- 1½ Tablespoon white granulated sugar

- 1½ teaspoon salt

- 1½ teaspoon bread machine yeast

Directions:

1. Soften the butter in your microwave.

2. Add each ingredient to the bread machine in the order and at the temperature recommended by your bread machine manufacturer.

3. Close the lid, select the basic or white bread, medium crust setting on your bread machine, and press start.

4. When the bread machine has finished baking, remove the bread and put it on a cooling rack.

Nutrition:

Carbs: 22 g

Fat: 1 g

Protein: 4 g

Calories: 104

Mom's White Bread

Preparation time: 5 minutes

Cooking time: 3 hours

Servings: 16

Difficulty : Beginners

Ingredients:

- 1 cup and 3 Tablespoon water

- 2 Tablespoon vegetable oil

- 1½ teaspoon salt

- 2 Tablespoon sugar

- 3¼ cups white bread flour

- 2 teaspoon active dry yeast

Directions:

1. Add each ingredient to the bread machine in the order and at the temperature recommended by your bread machine manufacturer.

2. Close the lid, select the basic or white bread, medium crust setting on your bread machine, and press start.

3. When the bread machine has finished baking, remove the bread and put it on a cooling rack.

Nutrition:

Carbs: 1 g

Fat: 3 g

Protein: 90 g

Calories: 74

Vegan White Bread

Preparation time: 5 minutes

Cooking time: 3 hours

Servings: 14

Difficulty : Beginners

Ingredients:

- 1 1/3 cups water

- 1/3 cup plant milk (I use silk soy original)

- 1½ teaspoon salt

- 2 Tablespoon granulated sugar

- 2 Tablespoon vegetable oil

- 3½ cups all-purpose flour

- 1¾ teaspoon bread machine yeast

Directions:

1. Add each ingredient to the bread machine in the order and at the temperature recommended by your bread machine manufacturer.

2. Close the lid, select the basic or white bread, medium crust setting on your bread machine, and press start.

3. When the bread machine has finished baking, remove the bread and put it on a cooling rack.

Nutrition:

Carbs: 13 g

Fat: 2 g

Protein: 3 g

Calories: 80

Rice Flour Rice Bread

Preparation time: 10 minutes

Cooking time: 3 hours 15 minutes

Servings: 16

Difficulty : Beginners

Ingredients:

- 3 eggs

- 1½ cups water

- 3 Tablespoon vegetable oil

- 1 teaspoon apple cider vinegar

- 2¼ teaspoon active dry yeast

- 3¼ cups white rice flour

- 2½ teaspoon xanthan gum

- 1½ teaspoon salt

- ½ cup dry milk powder

- 3 Tablespoon white sugar

Directions:

1. In a medium-size bowl, add the oil, water, eggs, and vinegar.

2. In a large dish, add the yeast, salt, xanthan gum, dry milk powder, rice flour, and sugar. Mix with a whisk until incorporated.

3. Add each ingredient to the bread machine in the order and at the temperature recommended by your bread machine manufacturer.

4. Close the lid, select the whole wheat, medium crust setting on your bread machine, and press start.

5. When the bread machine has finished baking, remove the bread and put it on a cooling rack.

Nutrition:

Carbs: 24 g

Fat: 1 g

Protein: 2 g

Calories: 95

Italian White Bread

Preparation time: 5 minutes

Cooking time: 3 hours

Servings: 14

Difficulty : Beginners

Ingredients:

- ¾ cup cold water

- 2 cups bread flour

- 1 Tablespoon sugar

- 1 teaspoon salt

- 1 Tablespoon olive oil

- 1 teaspoon active dry yeast

Directions:

1. Add each ingredient to the bread machine in the order and at the temperature recommended by your bread machine manufacturer.

2. Close the lid, select the Italian or basic bread, low crust setting on your bread machine, and press start.

3. When the bread machine has finished baking, remove the bread and put it on a cooling rack.

Nutrition:

Carbs: 11 g

Fat: 1 g

Protein: 2 g

Calories: 78

Anadama White Bread

Preparation time: 5 minutes

Cooking time: 3 hours

Servings: 14

Difficulty : Beginners

Ingredients:

- 1 1/8 cups water (110°F/43°C)

- 1/3 cup molasses

- 1½ Tablespoon butter at room temperature

- 1 teaspoon salt

- 1/3 cup yellow cornmeal

- 3½ cups bread flour

- 2½ teaspoon bread machine yeast

Directions:

1. Add each ingredient to the bread machine in the order and at the temperature recommended by your bread machine manufacturer.

2. Close the lid, select the basic bread, low crust setting on your bread machine, and press start.

3. When the bread machine has finished baking, remove the bread and put it on a cooling rack.

Nutrition:

Carbs: 19 g

Fat: 1 g

Protein: 2 g

Calories: 76

Soft White Bread

Preparation time: 5 minutes

Cooking time: 3 hours

Servings: 14

Difficulty : Beginners

Ingredients:

- 2 cups water

- 4 teaspoon yeast

- 6 Tablespoon sugar

- ½ cup vegetable oil

- 2 teaspoon salt

- 3 cups strong white flour

Directions:

1. Add each ingredient to the bread machine in the order and at the temperature recommended by your bread machine manufacturer.

2. Close the lid, select the basic bread, low crust setting on your bread machine, and press start.

3. When the bread machine has finished baking, remove the bread and put it on a cooling rack.

Nutrition:

Carbs: 18 g

Fat: 1 g

Protein: 4 g

Calories: 74

English muffin Bread recipe

Preparation time: 5 minutes

Cooking time: 3 hours 40 minutes

Servings: 14

Difficulty : Beginners

Ingredients:

- 1 teaspoon vinegar

- 1/4 to 1/3 cup water

- 1 cup lukewarm milk

- 2 Tablespoon butter or 2 Tablespoon vegetable oil

- 1½ teaspoon salt

- 1½ teaspoon sugar

- ½ teaspoon baking powder

- 3½ cups unbleached all-purpose flour

- 2 1/4 teaspoon instant yeast

Directions:

1. Add each ingredient to the bread machine in the order and at the temperature recommended by your bread machine manufacturer.

2. Close the lid, select the basic bread, low crust setting on your bread machine, and press start.

3. When the bread machine has finished baking, remove the bread and put it on a cooling rack.

Nutrition:

Carbs: 13 g

Fat: 1 g

Protein: 2 g

Calories: 62

Cranberry Orange Breakfast Bread

Preparation time: 5 minutes

Cooking time: 3 hours 10 minutes

Servings: 14

Difficulty : Beginners

Ingredients:

- 1 1/8 cup orange juice

- 2 Tablespoon vegetable oil

- 2 Tablespoon honey

- 3 cups bread flour

- 1 Tablespoon dry milk powder

- ½ teaspoon ground cinnamon

- ½ teaspoon ground allspice

- 1 teaspoon salt

- 1 (.25 ounce) package active dry yeast

- 1 Tablespoon grated orange zest

- 1 cup sweetened dried cranberries

- 1/3 cup chopped walnuts

Directions:

1. Add each ingredient to the bread machine in the order and at the temperature recommended by your bread machine manufacturer.

2. Close the lid, select the basic bread, low crust setting on your bread machine, and press start.

3. Add the cranberries and chopped walnuts 5 to 10 minutes before last kneading cycle ends.

4. When the bread machine has finished baking, remove the bread and put it on a cooling rack.

Nutrition:

Carbs: 29 g

Fat: 2 g

Protein: 9 g

Calories: 56

Buttermilk Honey Bread

Preparation time: 5 minutes

Cooking time: 3 hours 45 minutes

Servings: 14

Difficulty : Beginners

Ingredients:

- ½ cup water

- ¾ cup buttermilk

- ¼ cup honey

- 3 Tablespoon butter, softened and cut into pieces

- 3 cups bread flour

- 1½ teaspoon salt

- 2¼ teaspoon yeast (or 1 package)

Directions:

1. Add each ingredient to the bread machine in the order and at the temperature recommended by your bread machine manufacturer.

2. Close the lid, select the basic bread, medium crust setting on your bread machine and press start.

3. When the bread machine has finished baking, remove the bread and put it on a cooling rack.

Nutrition:

Carbs: 19 g

Fat: 1 g

Protein: 2 g

Calories: 92

Whole Wheat Breakfast Bread

Preparation time: 5 minutes

Cooking time: 3 hours 45 minutes

Servings: 14

Difficulty : Beginners

Ingredients:

- 3 cups white whole wheat flour

- ½ teaspoon salt

- 1 cup water

- ½ cup coconut oil, liquified

- 4 Tablespoon honey

- 2½ teaspoon active dry yeast

Directions:

1. Add each ingredient to the bread machine in the order and at the temperature recommended by your bread machine manufacturer.

2. Close the lid, select the basic bread, medium crust setting on your bread machine and press start.

3. When the bread machine has finished baking, remove the bread and put it on a cooling rack.

Nutrition:

Carbs: 11 g

Fat: 3 g

Protein: 1 g

Calories: 60

Cinnamon-Raisin Bread

Preparation time: 5 minutes

Cooking time: 3 hours

Servings: 4

Difficulty : Beginners

Ingredients:

- 1 cup water

- 2 Tablespoon butter, softened

- 3 cups Gold Medal Better for Bread flour

- 3 Tablespoon sugar

- 1½ teaspoon salt

- 1 teaspoon ground cinnamon

- 2½ teaspoon bread machine yeast

- ¾ cup raisins

Directions:

1. Add each ingredient except the raisins to the bread machine in the order and at the temperature recommended by your bread machine manufacturer.

2. Close the lid, select the sweet or basic bread, medium crust setting on your bread machine and press start.

3. Add raisins 10 minutes before the last kneading cycle ends.

4. When the bread machine has finished baking, remove the bread and put it on a cooling rack.

Nutrition:

Carbs: 38 g

Fat: 2 g

Protein: 4 g

Calories: 180

Butter Bread Rolls

Preparation time: 50 minutes

Cooking time: 45 minutes

Servings: 24 rolls

Difficulty : Beginners

Ingredients:

- 1 cup warm milk

- 1/2 cup butter or 1/2 cup margarine, softened

- 1/4 cup sugar

- 2 eggs

- 1 1/2 teaspoons salt

- 4 cups bread flour

- 2 1/4 teaspoons active dry yeast

Directions:

1 In bread machine pan, put all ingredients in order suggested by manufacturer.

2 Select dough setting.

3   When cycle is completed, turn dough onto a lightly floured surface.

4   Divide dough into 24 portions.

5   Shape dough into balls.

6   Place in a greased 13 inch by 9-inch baking pan.

7   Cover and let rise in a warm place for 30-45 minutes.

8   Bake at 350 degrees for 13-16 minutes or until golden brown.

Nutrition:

Carbs: 38 g

Fat: 2 g

Protein: 4 g

Calories: 180

Cranberry & Golden Raisin Bread

Preparation time: 5 minutes

Cooking time: 3 hours

Servings: 14

Difficulty : Beginners

Ingredients:

- 1 1/3 cups water

- 4 Tablespoon sliced butter

- 3 cups flour

- 1 cup old fashioned oatmeal

- 1/3 cup brown sugar

- 1 teaspoon salt

- 4 Tablespoon dried cranberries

- 4 Tablespoon golden raisins

- 2 teaspoon bread machine yeast

Directions:

1. Add each ingredient except cranberries and golden raisins to the bread machine one by one, according to the manufacturer's instructions.

2. Close the lid, select the sweet or basic bread, medium crust setting on your bread machine and press start.

3. Add the cranberries and golden raisins 5 to 10 minutes before the last kneading cycle ends.

4. When the bread machine has finished baking, remove the bread and put it on a cooling rack.

Nutrition:

Carbs: 33 g

Fat: 3 g

Protein: 4 g

Calories: 175

Sweet Bread

Buttery Sweet Bread

Preparation Time: 15 minutes,

Cooking Time: 3 hours,

Servings: 1 loaf

Ingredients:

- 1/3 cup water

- ½ cup milk

- ¼ cup sugar

- 1 beaten egg

- 1 teaspoon of salt

- ¼ cup margarine or ¼ cup butter

- 2 teaspoons bread machine yeast

- 3 1/3 cups bread flour

Directions:

- Put everything in your bread machine pan.

- Select the white bread setting.

- Take out the pan when done and set aside for 10 minutes.

Nutrition

Calories 168, Carbohydrates 28g, Total Fat 5g, Cholesterol 0mg, Protein 4g, Fiber 1g, Sugars 3g, Sodium 292mg, Potassium 50mg

Cinnamon Sugar Bread

Preparation Time: 15 minutes,

Cooking Time: 3 hours,

Servings: 1 loaf

Ingredients:

- ¼ cup margarine or ¼ cup softened butter

- 1 cup milk

- 3 cups of bread flour

- 1 egg

- ½ teaspoon of salt

- ½ cup sugar

- 2 teaspoons of yeast

- 1 1/4 teaspoons of cinnamon

Directions:

- Put everything in the pan of your bread machine.

- Select the white bread setting.

- Take it out when done and set aside for 10 minutes on a rack.

Nutrition

Calories 168, Carbohydrates 28g, Total Fat 5g, Cholesterol 0mg, Protein 4g, Fiber 1g, Sugars 3g, Sodium 292mg, Potassium 50mg

Chocolate Bread

Preparation Time: 10 minutes,

Cooking Time: 2 hours,

Servings: 1 loaf

Ingredients:

- 1 pack active dry yeast

- ½ cup sugar

- 3 cups bread flour

- 1/4 cup cocoa powder

- 1 large egg

- 1/4 cup butter

- ½ teaspoon vanilla extract

- 1 cup milk

Directions:

- Put everything in the pan of your bread machine.

- Select the quick bread or equivalent setting.

- Take out the pan when done and set aside for 10 minutes.

Nutrition

Calories 184, Carbohydrates 31g, Total Fat 5g, Cholesterol 13mg, Protein 5g, Fiber 2g, Sugar 8g, Sodium 214mg, Potassium 92mg

Cranberry Walnut Bread

Preparation Time: 10 minutes,

Cooking Time: 2 hours,

Servings: 1 loaf

Ingredients:

- ¼ cup water

- ¼ cup rolled oats

- 1 egg

- 1 cup buttermilk

- 1-1/2 tablespoons margarine

- 3 tablespoons honey

- 1 teaspoon salt

- 3 cups bread flour

- ½ teaspoon ground cinnamon

- ¼ teaspoon baking soda

- ¾ cup dried cranberries

- 2 teaspoons active dry yeast

- ½ cup chopped walnuts

Directions:

- Put everything in your bread machine pan, except the walnuts and cranberries.

- Set the machine to the light crust and the sweet cycle modes.

- Hit the start button.

- Add the walnuts and cranberries at the beep signal.

- Take out the pan when done and set aside for 10 minutes.

Nutrition

Calories 184, Carbohydrates 31g, Total Fat 5g, Cholesterol 13mg, Protein 5g, Fiber 2g, Sugar 8g, Sodium 214mg, Potassium 92mg

Coconut Ginger Bread

Preparation Time: 10 minutes,

Cooking Time: 2 hours,

Servings: 1 loaf

Ingredients:

- 1 cup + 2 tbsp Half & Half

- 1 ¼ cup toasted shredded coconut

- 2 large eggs

- ¼ cup oil

- 1 tsp coconut extract

- 1 tsp lemon extract

- 3/4 cup sugar

- 1 tbsp grated lemon peel

- 2 cups all-purpose flour

- 2 tbsp finely chopped candied ginger

- 1 tbsp baking powder

- ½ tsp salt

- 1 ¼ cup toasted shredded coconut

Directions:

- Put everything in your bread machine pan.

- Select the quick bread mode.

- Press the start button.

- Allow bread to cool on the wire rack until ready to serve (at least 20 minutes).

Nutrition

Calories 210, Carbohydrates 45g, Total Fat 3g, Cholesterol 3mg, Protein 5g, Fiber 2g, Sugar 15g, Sodium 185mg, Potassium 61mg

Easy Donuts

Preparation Time: 10 minutes,

Cooking Time: 2 hours,

Servings: 12

Ingredients:

- 2/3 cups milk, room temperature

- 1/4 cup water, room temperature

- ½ cup of warm water

- 1/4 cup softened butter

- 1 egg slightly beaten

- 1/4 cup granulated sugar

- 1 tsp salt

- 3 cups bread machine flour

- 2 1/2 tsp bread machine yeast

- oil for deep frying

- 1/4 cup confectioners' sugar

Directions:

- Place milk, water, butter, egg, sugar, salt, flour, and yeast into bread machine pan.

- Select dough setting and push start. Press the start button.

- When cycle is complete, remove dough from pan and transfer to lightly floured surface.

- Using rolling pin lightly dusted with flour, roll dough to ½ inch thickness.

- Cut with floured dusted donut cutter or circle cookie cutter.

- Transfer donuts to baking sheet that has been covered with wax paper. Place another layer of wax paper on top, then cover with clean tea towel. Let rise 30-40 minutes.

- Heat vegetable oil to 375º (190ºCº) in deep fryer or large heavy pot.

- Fry donuts 2-3 at a time until golden brown on both sides for about 3 minutes.

- Drain on paper towel.

- Sprinkle with confectioners' sugar.

Nutrition

Calories 180, Carbohydrates 30g, Total Fat 5g, Cholesterol 25mg, Protein 4g, Fiber 2g, Sugar 7g, Sodium 240mg, Potassium 64mg

Orange Bread

Preparation Time: 10 minutes,

Cooking Time: 3 hours,

Servings: 1 loaf

Ingredients:

- 1 cup orange juice

- 1 egg

- 1 tablespoon margarine

- ¼ cup hot water

- 3 1/2 cups bread flour

- ¼ cup white sugar

- 2 tablespoons orange zest

- 1 teaspoon salt

- 1 pack active dry yeast

Directions:

- Put all the ingredients in your bread machine pan according to the guidelines of the manufacturer.

- Select the machine's basic or white bread cycle.

- Press the start button.

- Take out the pan when done and set aside for 10 minutes.

Nutrition

Calories 210, Carbohydrates 45g, Total Fat 3g, Cholesterol 3mg, Protein 5g, Fiber 2g, Sugar 15g, Sodium 185mg, Potassium 61mg

Hawaiian Sweet Bread

Preparation Time: 10 minutes,

Cooking Time: 3 hours,

Servings: 1 loaf

Ingredients:

- ³/₄ cup pineapple juice

- 1 egg

- 2 tablespoons vegetable oil

- 2 ¹/₂ tablespoons honey

- ³/₄ teaspoon salt

- 3 cups bread flour

- 2 tablespoons dry milk

- 2 teaspoons fast rising yeast

Directions:

- Place ingredients in bread machine container.

- Select the white bread cycle.

- Press the start button.

- Take out the pan when done and set aside for 10 minutes.

Nutrition

Calories 169, Carbohydrates 25g, Total Fat 5g, Cholesterol 25mg, Protein 4g, Fiber 1g, Sugar 5g, Sodium 165mg, Potassium 76mg

Date and Nut Bread

Preparation Time: 10 minutes,

Cooking Time: 3 hours,

Servings: 1 loaf

Ingredients:

- 1-1/2 tablespoons vegetable oil

- 1 cup water

- ½ teaspoon salt

- 2 tablespoons honey

- ¾ cup whole-wheat flour

- ¾ cup rolled oats

- 1 1/2 teaspoons active dry yeast

- 1 1/2 cups bread flour

- ½ cup almonds, chopped

- ½ cup dates, chopped and pitted

Directions:

- Put everything in your bread machine pan.

- Select the basic cycle. Press the start button.

- Take out the pan when done and set aside for 10 minutes.

Nutrition

Calories 112, Carbohydrates 17g, Total Fat 5g, Cholesterol 0mg, Protein 3g, Fiber 3g, Sugar 7g, Sodium 98mg, Potassium 130mg

Peanut Butter and Jelly Bread

Preparation Time: 10 minutes,

Cooking Time: 3 hours,

Servings: 1 loaf

Ingredients:

- 1 1/2 tablespoons vegetable oil

- 1 cup of water

- ½ cup blackberry jelly

- ½ cup peanut butter

- 1 teaspoon salt

- 1 tablespoon white sugar

- 2 cups of bread flour

- 1 cup whole-wheat flour

- 1 1/2 teaspoons active dry yeast

Directions:

- Put everything in your bread machine pan.

- Select the basic setting.

- Press the start button.

- Take out the pan when done and set aside for 10 minutes.

Nutrition

Calories 153, Carbohydrates 20g, Total Fat 9g, Cholesterol 0mg, Protein 4g, Fiber 2g, Sugar 11g, Sodium 244mg, Potassium 120mg

Brown & White Sugar Bread

Preparation time: 5 minutes

Cooking time: 2 hours 55 minutes

Servings: 12

Difficulty : Intermediate

Ingredients:

- 1 cup milk (room temperature)

- ¼ cup butter, softened

- 1 egg

- ¼ cup light brown sugar

- ¼ cup granulated white sugar

- 2 tablespoons ground cinnamon

- ¼ teaspoon salt

- 3 cups bread flour

- 2 teaspoons bread machine yeast

Directions:

1. Place all ingredients in the baking pan of the bread machine in the order recommended by the manufacturer.

2. Place the baking pan in the bread machine and close the lid.

3. Select Sweet Bread setting and then Medium Crust.

4. Press the start button.

5. Carefully, remove the baking pan from the machine and then invert the bread loaf onto a wire rack to cool completely before slicing.

6. With a sharp knife, cut bread loaf into desired-sized slices and serve.

Nutrition:

Calories 195

Total Fat 5 g

Saturated Fat 2.8 g

Cholesterol 25 mg

Sodium 94 mg

Total Carbs 33.2 g

Fiber 1.6 g

Sugar 8.2 g

Protein 4.7 g

Molasses Bread

Preparation time: 5 minutes

Cooking time: 4 hours

Servings: 12

Difficulty : Intermediate

Ingredients:

- 1/3 cup milk

- ¼ cup water

- 3 tablespoons molasses

- 3 tablespoons butter, softened

- 2 cups bread flour

- 1¾ cups whole-wheat flour

- 2 tablespoons white sugar

- 1 teaspoon salt

- 2¼ teaspoons quick-rising yeast

Directions:

1. Place all ingredients in the baking pan of the bread machine in the order recommended by the manufacturer.

2. Place the baking pan in the bread machine and close the lid.

3. Select light browning setting.

4. Press the start button.

5. Carefully, remove the baking pan from the machine and then invert the bread loaf onto a wire rack to cool completely before slicing.

6. With a sharp knife, cut bread loaf into desired-sized slices and serve.

Nutrition:

Calories 205

Total Fat 3.9 g

Saturated Fat 1.9 g

Cholesterol 8 mg

Sodium 220 mg

Total Carbs 37.4 g

Fiber 3.1 g

Sugar 5.1 g

Protein 5.6 g

Honey Bread

Preparation time: 5 minutes

Cooking time: 2 hours

Servings: 16

Difficulty : Intermediate

Ingredients:

- 1 cup plus 1 tablespoon milk

- 3 tablespoons honey

- 3 tablespoons butter, melted

- 3 cups bread flour

- 1½ teaspoons salt

- 2 teaspoons active dry yeast

Directions:

1. Place all ingredients in the baking pan of the bread machine in the order recommended by the manufacturer.

2. Place the baking pan in the bread machine and close the lid.

3. Select White Bread setting and then Medium Crust.

4. Press the start button.

5. Carefully, remove the baking pan from the machine and then invert the bread loaf onto a wire rack to cool completely before slicing.

6. With a sharp knife, cut bread loaf into desired-sized slices and serve.

Nutrition:

Calories 126

Total Fat 2.7 g

Saturated Fat 1.6 g

Cholesterol 70 mg

Sodium 241 mg

Total Carbs 22.1 g

Fiber 0.8 g

Sugar 4 g

Protein 3.2 g

Maple Syrup Bread

Preparation time: 5 minutes

Cooking time: 3 hours

Servings: 12

Difficulty : Intermediate

Ingredients:

- 1 cup buttermilk

- 2 tablespoons maple syrup

- 2 tablespoons vegetable oil

- 2 tablespoons non-fat dry milk powder

- 1 cup whole-wheat flour

- 2 cups bread flour

- 1 teaspoon salt

- 1½ teaspoons bread machine yeast

Directions:

1. Place all ingredients in the baking pan of the bread machine in the order recommended by the manufacturer.

2. Place the baking pan in the bread machine and close the lid.

3. Select Basic setting.

4. Press the start button.

5. Carefully, remove the baking pan from the machine and then invert the bread loaf onto a wire rack to cool completely before slicing.

6. With a sharp knife, cut bread loaf into desired-sized slices and serve.

Nutrition:

Calories 151

Total Fat 2.6 g

Saturated Fat 0.6 g

Cholesterol 1 mg

Sodium 217 mg

Total Carbs 26.1 g

Fiber 0.4 g

Sugar 3.8 g

Protein 4.7 g

Peanut Butter & Jelly Bread

Preparation time: 5 minutes

Cooking time: 3 hours

Servings: 12

Difficulty : Intermediate

Ingredients:

- 1 cup water

- 1½ tablespoons vegetable oil

- ½ cup peanut butter

- ½ cup blackberry jelly

- 1 tablespoon white sugar

- 1 teaspoon salt

- 1 cup whole-wheat flour

- 2 cups bread flour

- 1½ teaspoons active dry yeast

Directions:

1. Place all ingredients in the baking pan of the bread machine in the order recommended by the manufacturer.

2. Place the baking pan in the bread machine and close the lid.

3. Select Sweet Bread setting.

4. Press the start button.

5. Carefully, remove the baking pan from the machine and then invert the bread loaf onto a wire rack to cool completely before slicing.

6. With a sharp knife, cut bread loaf into desired-sized slices and serve.

Nutrition:

Calories 218

Total Fat 7.2 g

Saturated Fat 1.5 g

Cholesterol 0 mg

Sodium 245 mg

Total Carbs 31.6 g

Fiber 1.1 g

Sugar 2.7 g

Protein 6.7 g

Lightning Source UK Ltd.
Milton Keynes UK
UKHW052131250221
379245UK00007B/15

9 781802 086461